HERE'S A SAMPLE OF SOME OF THE MANY USES FOR THE UGLY JOKE BOOK

NOW *there's a way to let someone know the truth about themselves:*

> Beauty is only skin deep, but UGLY goes all the way down . . .

GET BACK *at the louse who dumped you—fill her in on some hard facts:*

> One day she discovered a great birth control device—*HER FACE!*

A GIFT *for somebody who has everything—but good looks!*

> He was so ugly, when he was born his mother was arrested for littering!

BEING UGLY ISN'T SO BAD, LOOK WHAT IT DID FOR E.T.!

ATTENTION: SCHOOLS AND CORPORATIONS

PINNACLE Books are available at quantity discounts with bulk purchases for educational, business or special promotional use. For further details, please write to: SPECIAL SALES MANAGER, Pinnacle Books, Inc., 1430 Broadway, New York, NY 10018.

WRITE FOR OUR FREE CATALOG

If there is a Pinnacle Book you want—and you cannot find it locally—it is available from us simply by sending the title and price plus 75¢ to cover mailing and handling costs to:

> Pinnacle Books, Inc.
> Reader Service Department
> 1430 Broadway
> New York, NY 10018

Please allow 6 weeks for delivery.

_____Check here if you want to receive our catalog regularly.

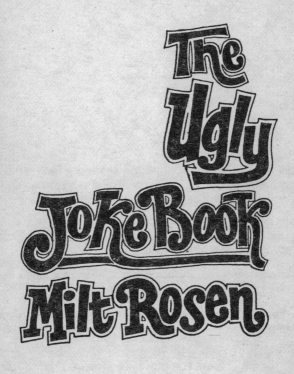

PINNACLE BOOKS   NEW YORK

This is a work of fiction. All the characters and events portrayed in this book are fictional, and any resemblance to real people or incidents is purely coincidental.

THE UGLY JOKE BOOK

Copyright © 1982 by Milt Rosen

All rights reserved, including the right to reproduce this book or portions thereof in any form.

An original Pinnacle Books edition, published for the first time anywhere.

First printing, December 1982

ISBN: 0-523-41808-6

Cover illustration by Scott Ross

Printed in the United States of America

PINNACLE BOOKS, INC.
1430 Broadway
New York, New York 10018

This book is dedicated to all the blemishes in the world

Buy this book and insult a close friend

INTRODUCTION

"Beautiful" is not funny. It never has been. Only the flawed is funny. The first joke proves that. Adam woke up to find this woman at his side. He said, "Who are you?" She said, "I'm your rib." He said, "You're not all you're cracked up to be."

Only the imperfect is funny. Adam, seeing Eve, would get no laugh telling her how pretty she was or how well she looked. He would have to complain, "I hate that outfit you're wearing. Can't you turn over a new leaf?"

Because sources of humor were limited in Paradise—after all, who can be hysterical about a kumquat?—Adam started to bitch about his wife's looks. She bitched back. And "ugly" jokes were born, to be followed in short order by "fat" jokes, "skinny" jokes, "tall" jokes, "short" jokes, and other jokes about abnormalities. They continue unabated.

Compiled and written by a man obsessed with the ugly, this volume is the largest collection of "ugly" jokes ever assembled. At a cost of about three for a penny, it is the biggest bargain since free plague.

Used properly, it can also bring a divorce.

"It's me, Walter. It's me."

She was so ugly, when she went to a plastic surgeon, it had to be a blind date.

* * *

She was so ugly, when she went to her gynecologist, he examined her through a rear-view mirror.

* * *

He was so ugly, he helped women diet. When he got undressed they lost their appetites.

* * *

"My girl just slipped into something more comfortable."
"What was that?"
"A telephone booth."

When she walked into a restaurant, they gave her a doggie bag <u>before</u> she ate.

* * *

"Why don't you take your wife on a second honeymoon?"
"What for? Her looks loused up the first one."

* * *

"My wife is a cab driver."
"A lady cab driver?"
"Yeah, if you look close."

* * *

"Does your wife get around much?"
"She's out a lot."
"What places does she haunt the most?"
"Our apartment when she gets up in the morning."

One day she discovered a great birth control device . . . her face.

* * *

She was so ugly, when she went to see "The Wizard of Oz," she rooted for the witches.

* * *

She was so ugly, when she went to the altar, nobody believed it was for marriage. They thought she was going to be ordained.

* * *

She was so fat, she could eat a Safeway.

* * *

Her measurements were 55-46-44. Her other breast was just a little smaller.

She was so fat, she went on her honeymoon in a U-Haul.

* * *

He was so short, he could read dice from below.

* * *

A lecherous wrinkled old man happened by a young lady in the park. "Where have you been all my life?" he asked. She answered, "For the first two-thirds of it I wasn't born yet."

* * *

She was so fat, it took a couple of tugs to get her out of her slip.

"One day my wife ate a hundred and ten candy bars."
"What happened?"
"She broke out with a twenty-eight pound pimple."

No one really knew how wide her mouth was until they saw her eat a fried egg with a knife.

* * *

She was so ugly, she could make a mule back away from an oat bin.

* * *

She was so fat, she had to bathe in a rubber tub.

* * *

Even her eyes were fat. She had to bat her eyelids by hand.

* * *

His nose was so big, it had its own zip code.

She was so ugly, the stork who was delivering her waited around until dark.

* * *

He had a map only Rand McNally could love.

* * *

She was so bowlegged, they hung her her over the door for good luck.

* * *

He was so thin, he had to use his Adam's apple as a chin.

* * *

She had a complexion like whipped cream, and her nose looked like it was the beater.

He was so thin, he had to use his Adam's apple to hold up his pants.

* * *

I'll never forget Old Paint. Old Paint, that's my wife.

* * *

She was so ugly, her parents put out a contract on her.

* * *

He was so ugly, eight years after he was born his parents were still trying to get a legal abortion.

* * *

He was so ugly, customs made him put somebody else's picture on his passport.

She won a beauty contest hands down. The judges took another look at her and put their hands up again.

* * *

His face was so pockmarked he shaved with an ice cream scoop.

* * *

He was so hairy, he didn't have to wear clothes. When he went somewhere he just buttoned up his body.

She had a beautiful face, except for her nose. She had to lift it to eat.

* * *

She was a perfect "10." Her face was a two, her body was a two, her legs were a two . . .

* * *

She was a perfect "10". These were her dimensions—ten, ten and ten.

* *

Her breasts were so small, she had to carry her nipples in her pocket.

* * *

She didn't have a hair on her head. She was a platinum bald.

She had police beauty; she could stop traffic..

* * *

Her face was like a road map—lots of folds.

* * *

Her face sticking out of a cellar door could start a hockey game.

* * *

Her looks were always discussed ... or was it disgust?

* * *

She had beautiful eyes. It was a shame she had three of them.

One good lipstick brought out her lips. One good sneeze brought out her teeth.

* * *

He had affectionate eyes—one always kept looking at the other.

* * *

Her mouth was so big, she could play the tuba from either end.

* * *

He worshipped the ground she crawled out of.

* * *

She had her face lifted so many times, she finally had "Welcome Home" written under her eyebrows.

A young man, for some strange reason, fell in love with a very ugly young lady. He begged her to marry him. He said, "If you don't marry me, I'll die." He was a man of his word. She didn't marry him. Sixty-six years later he died.

* * *

She was so ugly, she tried out for a job as a hooker at the Mustang Ranch and was beaten out by a mustang.

* * *

She took off her false hair, her false eyelashes, her falsies, her false teeth, and her gentlemen friend yelled out, "One more false move and I'm getting out of here!"

The ugliest man married the ugliest woman in the world. After a year of marriage, she gave birth to a baby. The baby was beautiful with gorgeous dimples, long blonde hair, and blue eyes. Seeing his baby for the first time, Mr. Ugly said to his wife, "Where did we go wrong?"

* * *

She had warts all over her body. That's why flies never bothered her. They could never find the right spot.

* * *

One day an ugly hag was captured by Arabian slave dealers. She was sold to a chieftain who wanted to give her as a gift to the big sheik. He caravanned to the sheik's oasis and presented the ugly woman. "Here," he said, "is a little present."

The sheik looked at the hag and said, "Present? She looks more like past tents."

She was so ugly, they had to buy her back from the dog catcher eight times.

* * *

She was a vision in the evening ... and a sight in the morning.

* * *

"You never take me on trips."
"Why should I? With a map like yours."

* * *

"He was so cross-eyed, he had to go to school in the Southeast to join the Northwest Mounties."

* * *

"She's so fat, she should diet."
"Really? What color would help?"

She was so ugly, blackheads had *her*.

* * *

"My wife went to a health farm."
"How's she doing?"
"She lost half her weight in two weeks."
"How much longer do you want her to stay?"
"Another two weeks."

* * *

She had the face of a saint ... a Saint Bernard.

* * *

"How do you get a pair of new teeth like that?"
"You go into somebody's back yard and kick a strange dog."

"How old do you think I am?"
"Gee, you don't look that old."

* * *

She tried to improve her looks with vitamins. At night she rubbed her whole body with Vitamin E. When she went to sleep she kept sliding out of bed.

* * *

She took tons of iron because it was good for the complexion. One day she got caught in the rain and came up with a new color—rust!

* * *

"Are you unattached?"
"No, I'm just put together sloppy."

Her feet were so big, her toes had to get their own shoes.

* * *

She was so flat, her hope chest was a training bra.

* * *

She once put on a living bra. It died.

* * *

She was so fat, one day she went to a Big Man's Shop, but they wouldn't sell her one.

He was so fat, his high school year book picture was on pages 34, 35, and 36.

* * *

His chins were like a serial—to be continued.

* * *

He had so many chins, when he drooled, people honeymooned nearby.

* * *

"I haven't seen my wife in a month."
"Do you miss her?"
"Not yet."

* * *

He was so ugly, he always wore a mask. Except when he robbed a bank.

"What does your girl look like?"
"Take the face of Sophia Loren, the body of Valerie Perrine, the bosom of Jacqueline Bisset, and the eyes of Jane Fonda. What you have left, that's my girl."

* * *

"Don't move," he said. "I want to forget you just the way you are."

* * *

"My girl is having her portrait painted by Rembrandt."
"Rembrandt's dead."
"A job like that would kill anybody.

* * *

"My wife's at home alone."
"Isn't that kind of risky, with prowlers and kidnappers and rapists everywhere?"
"Well, if you tke up that line of work, you have to take risks."

"You keep making fun of your girl's looks. Is her face ugly? Her shape? Her legs? Her nose?"
"Yes."
"Doesn't she have one good point?"
"Her head."

* * *

"Your wife has a double chin?"
"Yeah, it was too much for one."

* * *

A mother walked into her twenty-year old daughter's room and was horrified to find her daughter, a very ugly young woman, in bed with a handsome young man. His figure was lithe and muscular. His handsome face had finely chiseled features. Upset, the mother demanded to know what was going on.

"I can explain everything, mother," the daughter said. "I was coming home last night. While passing the pond, I heard this little frog croaking. I leaned over and he said, 'Miss, I'm a prince. An ugly spell has turned

me into a frog. If you kiss me, I'll turn into a prince again.' I brought him home and put him on my night stand, but he kept begging for me to kiss him. So about an hour ago I kissed him. You see what happened."

The mother said, "If he wasn't green, I wouldn't believe you."

* * *

An ugly bride started to discuss plans with her husband. "Let's not stay home all the time," she said. "Let's go out at least three times a week."

Her husband answered, "Great. You go out Monday, Wednesday and Friday. I'll go out Tuesday, Thursday and Saturday."

* * *

"If you felt I was ugly, why did you marry me?"
"I wanted to stop dating ugly girls."

The plastic surgeon couldn't help her improve her looks, but he did perform one human service. He tattooed "BEWARE" on her forehead.

* * *

He finally discovered a way to overcome his wife's ugliness. He kept getting jobs farther and farther out of town.

* * *

She looked like a maidmer . . . that's like a mermaid except the top half is a fish.

* * *

She looked like stale beer . . . no head.

She wasn't just ugly, she was cheap. She once got acne because it was free.

* * *

She was so ugly, at smart parties they asked her to snort Gainsburgers.

* * *

She had more chins that a Chinese phonebook.

* * *

He was so fat as a child, when it started to rain they made him come into the house so the lawn could get wet.

He was so fat, every time he went through a turnstile he had to make three trips.

* * *

She was so fat, she looked like a parade standing still.

* * *

She was so ugly, when she posed for a photographer who said, "Watch the birdie," the birdie wouldn't come out.

* * *

She was so bowlegged, she looked like two giraffes kissing.

Her legs looked like Napoleon . . . two boney parts.

* * *

He was so thin, when he wore a double-breasted jacket, he had to button it in the back.

* * *

She was so cross-eyed, she could look through a keyhole with both eyes.

* * *

He was so skinny, when he stood sideways in school, he was marked absent.

She had one tooth, but it came in handy ... for opening beer bottles.

* * *

"She had her face lifted the other day."
"Yeah. Who took it?"

* * *

"What have you got against your wife?"
"Have you ever seen her?"
"No."
"That's it. She looks like something you've never seen."

* * *

"Your wife is not a sex pot?"
"She's got the pot. Now she's working on the rest of it."

She was so ugly, when he took her to the movies he had to pay an abusement tax.

* * *

"Your wife looks a little on the heavy side."
"She's heavy on every side."

* * *

"If you're not too thrilled with your wife, why did you marry her?"
"In a moment of weakness, I kissed her and forces stronger than myself told me to propose."
"Emotions can do that."
"Emotions, hell. It was her father and two giant brothers."

* * *

She was so bony, they used to x-ray her for meat.

Her feet had an immeasurable beauty. After 23 triple D, you stop counting.

* * *

"I can't believe that your wife has a beard."
"That's what I say every night when she's shaving."

* * *

It's very difficult for a man to be ugly, but he tries very hard.

* * *

She used tons of makeup until one night her boyfriend, bugged by the mess, dragged her down to the cosmetics factory. "See," he said, "no matter how much you use they can make more." She said, "I know, but I've got them working nights."

"That's my girl. You just saw her in the flesh."
"Couldn't she get a better fitting?"

* * *

People thought she had bags under her eyes. Actually she was just wearing her cheeks up that season.

* * *

"Do you have a trade?"
"Yeah, my wife for anything you got."

* * *

She had a stiff upper lip. She brushed her teeth with starch.

One time she went to Florida for her looks. But they weren't there.

* * *

He was so ugly, when he was a kid they made him poster boy for birth control.

* * *

She had a scar that started at her temple, ran down her cheek, down her jaw, and across the room to her sister.

* * *

A plastic surgeon once told her that plastic surgery for her would be like getting a kidney transplant for a bedwetter.

"She has very extinguished looks."
"You mean 'distinguished.'"
"No, extinguished. She should be put out."

* * *

Both she and her husband were very fat. On their honeymoon night they decided they were seeing too much of each other.

* * *

She was so ugly, they hired a professional child actress to play her in home movies.

* * *

Her feet were so big, she rented herself to the forest service for stamping out fires.

She looked like an accident going someplace to happen.

* * *

"She has a face that only a mother can love."
"Not necessarily. I'm her mother."

* * *

She was such an ugly bride, after the ceremony everybody got in line to kiss the groom.

* * *

She was so ugly, they decided to tar and feather her until somebody got up and said, "If she wants to improve her looks, let her do it by herself."

She looked like an escaped pimple.

* * *

He was such an ugly baby, his folks sued the sperm bank.

* * *

He was such an ugly baby, his father went to court to have his vasectomy made retroactive.

* * *

Her looks were made in Heaven, which may explain why the Lord decided to take a day off.

* * *

She looked like a great canvas . . . oily.

Her face could launch a thousand ships. When she came around, the marina emptied.

* * *

Men drank to her face. They had to.

* * *

When she came to the beauty parlor, her beautician sang to her . . . "The Impossible Dream."

* * *

No one knew she had an upper plate till it came out in the conversation.

* * *

Motto of her bra company: "What Nature's Forgotten, We Stuff With Cotton."

He was so ugly, when he tried to put on runproof socks, they ran.

* * *

She had so many cavities in her teeth, she talked with an echo.

* * *

One day, dressed in blue, she walked down the street and yawned. Somebody shoved a letter in her mouth.

* * *

She got her looks from her father. He was a plastic surgeon.

* * *

She had a face like a flower . . . a cauliflower.

Her calves were so fat, they mooed.

* * *

This woman is walking along with a duck under her arm. A drunk who is passing by stops and says, "Where'd you get that pig?"
"Sir, that happens to be a duck."
"I know. I was talking to the duck."

* * *

She had a face like a dog's dinner.

* * *

He was so fat, when he sat down on a barstool, he had a hangover before drinking.

* * *

Her bust was so large, she had to back up to ring a doorbell.

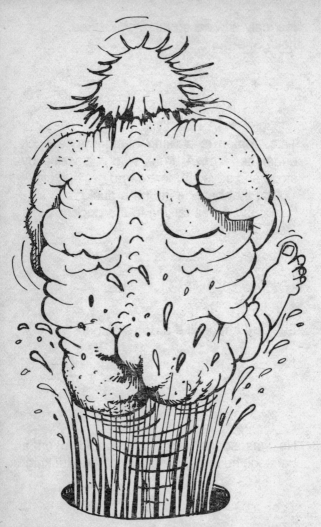

She worked for the flood control people. When they had a problem, she would sit down and stand up real quick over clogged manholes to clear them.

One day her boyfriend took her to a dog show. She won.

* * *

She was so ugly, her canary flew around in its cage with one wing over its eyes.

* * *

Her knees were very affectionate. She couldn't keep them apart.

* * *

She wasn't exactly fat. She was just a little broad-shouldered around the belt.

* * *

Nobody ever saw anybody as ugly as him without paying admission.

"I wish I had sore eyes."
"Why?"
"You'd be a sight for them."

* * *

She's so fat, she hates to sit down. She can't stand high places.

* * *

She has so much hair on her face, when she shaves street lights dim.

* * *

Her first husband was a judge. That's what people thought until he married her.

* * *

She had a faraway look about her. Far away she looked okay.

She's a treasure. She looks like something they dug up.

* * *

She was so fat, when a shoe clerk told her her shoe size, she had to take his word for it.

* * *

She looks like a page out of *Vogue*. In fact, nobody is more out of vogue than she is.

* * *

She had a certain something that would turn a man's head . . . and his stomach too.

* * *

She was like a bus that stopped at a liquor store. She drove men to drink.

Her face had everything ... including four or five things that have never been seen on faces before.

* * *

Have you ever heard the song "You'll Never Walk Alone?" She had to.

* * *

She had an olive complexion ... pits and all.

* * *

He wanted to take her hand in marriage, but he found out he'd have to take the rest of her too.

She had very big feet. She was taller lying down than standing up.

"Will you take my hand in marriage?"
"That would leave you only one."

*   *   *

"Do you take this woman for your lawfully wedded wife?"
"If I have a choice, there's a girl three rows back I could be interested in."

*   *   *

She looked like death warmed over . . . in a waffle iron.

*   *   *

Everybody said she was one of the boys. That's because she looked like one.

Her eyes were like a baseball game ... a two bagger.

* * *

She was so fat when she hung around the corner, cops came along and said, "Break it up."

* * *

She was so fat, when she passed a drugstore, the scales inside jumped.

* * *

When she walked into a bank, they'd turn off the camera.

She was so ugly, when she was captured by cannibals, they threw her away and cooked her clothes.

* * *

She was a luscious-looking woman. Only lushes would look at her.

* * *

She was like a song—"The Wreck of the Old '97."

* * *

Her looks were bountiful. Unfortunately she couldn't find any bounty hunters.

* * *

The easiest way to find the ugliest girl in town—Ask somebody to get you a blind date.

She was so ugly, in school she was chosen as the Most Likely to be the Least Likely.

* * *

She was so ugly, she could model for death threats.

* * *

Men liked to needle her; she looked like one.

* * *

She was so crossed-eyed, when she rolled her eyes she'd hit her ears.

* * *

Everybody knew she would get ahead ... the one she had was terrible.

A man was a terrible drunkard, so one day to frighten him his wife dressed up in a skin and bones costume and hid behind the door. When he came in, she jumped from behind the door.

"Who are you?" he asked.

"I am death and I've come to warn you."

"Nice meeting you. You know, I married your sister."

She had so many chins, she had to jack up her face to wash it.

* * *

She was such an ugly child that one day her father took her aside and left her there.

* * *

This very ugly woman happened to be in a store when a robber pulled a gun and demanded all the cash. If he didn't get his money he would rape all the women. One woman said, "You wouldn't dare!"

The ugly one looked at her, "Shut up, you're not robbing this store."

* * *

She's so ugly I understand they use her picture to make foreign spies confess.

"Who cares if she's ugly. Beauty is only skin deep."
"Good, let's skin her."

* * *

"She says that her figure is sylphlike."
"I don't argue with her. It's just that I never saw a big fat sylph."

* * *

Even the most beautiful woman fades with time. Can you imagine what happens to the ugly ones?

* * *

She had so many facelifts, there was nothing left in her shoes.

When caught with a very ugly woman, this sailor said "Look, it's getting late at night. So I say any port in a storm."

"But did you have to find one whose pier was dragging?"

Worried sick by the fact that he was unable to look at his wife because of her ugliness, a man went to his parish priest. "Father," he said, "I tried to take it for years, but it's become impossible now. She's so ugly. What can I do?"

The parish priest thought for a moment then said, "On the way home tonight, pick up a couple of oozy slimy snails and keep them in the house with you."

The husband walked home. Passing a dewy field, he gathered a few of the ooziest and slimiest snails he could find. He brought them into the house and put them on his mantlepiece.

A few days later, he returned to the priest. "Father, I don't know what kind of hocus-pocus you had in mind, but I looked at my wife and I got weak in the knees."

The priest said, "Go to the caves outside of town and collect a few bats. Keep them in the house too."

The man did as he was told. Again, he returned to the priest in a few days. "I got some bats," he said. "I got some bats," he said. Still no help."

The priest said, "Go to the pond and pick up a half dozen toads. They go inside the house too."

The man did as bid, but came to the priest again in a matter of days. "It's impossible in my house with those slimy, ugly creatures. Worse still, I looked at my wife and I almost gagged."

The priest said, "All right, stare at them a while."

The man did so. In a few days he returned to the priest. "You worked a miracle, Father. I stared at snails and the bats and the toads. Then I looked at my wife. You have no idea how pretty she's become."

* * *

She was so fat, they had to feed her with a harpoon.

* * *

She was so thin they once took an x-ray of her chest and missed.

* * *

He had so many pockmarks on his face, he shaved with an echo.

She had so much hair on her face, her electric razor had three speeds—Slow, Fast, and Timber.

* * *

She was so ugly, she went to the beauty parlor out of memory.

* * *

She had beautiful long black hair . . . under her armpits.

* * *

She had a natural complexion . . . oatmeal.

* * *

The ugly wife wasn't feeling too well. Her husband took her to the family physician who gave her a complete physical. He could find nothing wrong physically and concluded, "Your wife feels unloved. She must have sex at least ten times a month." The husband shrugged, "Okay, doc, put me down for two."

* * *

A woman was sitting on a bus. In her arms was cradled the ugliest baby on earth. The man sitting next to the woman tried not to look at the child, but his eyes kept drifting to the horrible-looking youngster.

Finally, unable to contain himself, the man said, "Lady, that is the ugliest kid I ever saw. It looks like you threw away the baby and kept the afterbirth. Just looking at it makes me ill."

When they came to the next bus stop, the woman, shattered by the man's words, got off the bus and stood at the bus stop, shaking and crying.

A policeman walked over. Seeing how upset the woman was, he said, "You need something to drink." He rushed into a store and came out a few moments later. "Here," he said, "here's a glass of water for you. And I brought some peanuts for your monkey."

In this rather plain restaurant, one of the busboys was much less than handsome. His face was long and lean, his hair was scraggly and hung down in clotted braids. He was not attractive.

A customer came in for a sandwich and stared at the busboy. The busboy became a little nervous and asked the man why he was staring. The man answered, "About twenty years ago when I was out here in the west, I made love to a buffalo one night. I was wondering if you could be my kid."

* * *

When she went to a dance, instead of being a wallflower, she was a wall weed.

* * *

For a long time, she felt she was ugly. Somebody told her to become more positive. Now she's positive she's ugly.

She was so ugly when she was born, for the first six months they diapered the wrong end.

A man was cast adrift and finally ended up on a deserted island. For fifteen years, he was without the companionship of a woman. One day he found a bottle. Taking a piece of cloth from his shirt he scribbled a note, sealed it in the bottle, and threw it in the ocean. The bottle drifted for five years and was finally picked up by a very ugly woman. Because the note seemed so urgent, she hired a yacht and headed for that island. She presented herself to the lonesome castaway. "Here I am," she said. "I got your message." The castaway looked at her. "It must have come from that next island."

* * *

She was so ugly, she wasn't listed in Who's Who. She was listed in What's that?

* * *

She always went around with a chip on her shoulder—her head.

"Take your pick."

"With her looks she could go far."
"Why doesn't she?"

* * *

"I hear your wife went around braless the other day."
"She certainly did."
"Did you notice anything?"
"Her neck straightened out."

* * *

"She felt a lump in her breast. It was her shoe."

* * *

A peeping tom looked in her window one night and the next day sent her money for drapes.

"She loves blind dates."
"Why?"
"They can't tell how ugly she is."

His wife was, to put it mildly, unattractive, but he'd been taught that it's what's underneath that counted. So he carried one of her x-rays in his wallet.

* * *

"I'm gonna marry an ugly girl, because a good-looking girl could run away."
"An ugly girl could run away."
"Yeah, but who would care?"

* * *

"I'm going down tomorrow to get a dog for my wife."
"If you can make it, that's a good trade."

* * *

She was so ugly, she lit up a room when she left it.

Women like her don't grow on trees. They swing from them.

* * *

She was born twins, but her mother must have thrown the good one away.

* * *

One day she went to a bar. When she sat down, five guys took the pledge.

* * *

She had bobbed hair. On her chin.

* * *

"My wife is a dear. And I can't wait for the hunting season to start."

He took his girl to the zoo, but the zoo wouldn't accept her.

* * *

"I hear your ugly sister got married."
"Yup."
"Who's the lucky man?"
"My father."

* * *

She always kept her mouth closed. She was afraid they'd put an apple in it.

* * *

A very ugly girl lucked into marriage with a handsome young man. Her father was so grateful, he told the son-in-law, "I appreciate what you did and I love you for it. To show you how I feel, I'm going to give you half of my business. And is there anything else I can do for you?"

She had so many pimples on her face, other kids loved her. They could play connect the dots.

The young man answered without thinking, "Buy me out!"

* * *

One day she had a nose operation. She had it put between her eyes.

* * *

A house of ill repute was famous for the beauty of many of its young ladies. A customer, new to the establishment, spent a rather long period of time choosing from one of the many beauties paraded before him. Finally he opted for one who had the classic beauty of a movie star. Walking with her toward the steps that would take them to her chambers and thus bliss, the customer happened to notice a young trollop in a corner. She was as ugly as sin. Her face was filled with blemishes, her nose looked as if it had been hit by a bus, her bosom was nonexistent; she was at best a zero in the rating game. But the customer felt a pang in his heart for the unfortunate young girl. It would be an incredible act of mercy if he chose her. He excused himself from the vivacious whore and presented himself to the ugly one. They went upstairs to her room. As she started to undress, the girl started to moan, "Why does it always have to be me?"

* * *

She's dark and beautiful . . . I mean, when it's dark, she's beautiful.

* * *

She was so ugly she could make a hurricane hiccup.

* * *

One out of three people in the world is born ugly. There is a foolproof way of finding out if you're that one. Look to your right, then look to your left. If both sides are looking at you, you're the one.

She used to wear a sign—This side up in case of rape.

Beauty is only skin deep, but ugly goes all the way down.

* * *

A man was married to a wealthy but extremely unattractive woman. On a cruise, as they stood on deck, a strong wave slapped into the ship causing the woman to slip and fall in the water.

Another passenger rushed to the husband, saying, "Your wife fell into the water." The husband said, "If she doesn't make it back in a couple of hours, we'll call somebody."

* * *

On another cruise, this wife wasn't merely ugly, she was also a nonstop talker. She badgered her husband without end. She talked in the cabin, she talked at meals, she talked on deck. Talk, talk, talk. As they were standing on deck, she slipped and fell into the water. A passenger rushed to her husband, "Your wife fell in the water."

"Thank God," the husband answered, "I thought I was going deaf."

She was so fat, she used to go to the desert and sell shade.

* * *

She went in for a three-week diet and lost twenty-one days.

* * *

She bought a beautiful dress for a ridiculous figure. Hers.

* *

"I got my girl something she can't get into."
"Get her another dress."
"What dress? It's a Volkswagen."

* * *

An ugly girl was being mugged. Finally, the mugger said, "You have no money on you." The ugly answered, "Keep doing what you're doing, I'll write you a check."

He was not fat. He was just short for his weight. He should have been 8'6".

* * *

She's ugly but she's neat. Every wrinkle is in place.

* * *

He was so fat, when he bought a sports car, they had to let out the doors.

* * *

A man goes to visit an acquaintance and the door is opened by a very ugly woman. The man asks his acquaintance, "Is that your wife?"

"Of course, it's my wife. Would I have a maid that ugly?"

"He has the face of a movie star."
"When the movie star finds out what he's doing with it, he'll kill him."

* * *

Even though she lived in the toughest part of town, she was so ugly, her rape whistle had rust on it.

* * *

She applied for rape insurance, but the company wouldn't send anybody.

* * *

She didn't look like an old maid. She looked more like an old un-made.

She had terrible buck teeth. She could eat corn through a Venetian blind.

* * *

She went to a plastic surgeon for a face lift. It was too much work so he just lowered her body.

* * *

She was very ugly but she could have married anybody she pleased. Unfortunately, she didn't please anybody.

* * *

She was so thin, when she wanted to turn sideways, she didn't have to move.

Men threw themselves at her feet. They couldn't stand her face.

* * *

She looked like a million dollars—all green and crumpled.

* * *

She was so ugly, she wore a veil, to no avail.

* * *

One day somebody said she was uglier than sin. Sin sued.

* * *

"Mirror, mirror, what shall I do with my face?"
"Get shatterproof glass."

Men always had to look at her twice. They didn't believe her the first time.

* * *

A man was walking down the street with his fiancée when he ran into an old friend. They went into a restaurant for a cup of coffee. Taking a moment, when the young lady was looking the other way, the friend whispered, "Where did you find this mess? She's the ugliest thing I ever saw. Her nose, her lips, her eyes—ugly! The man smiled, "You don't have to whisper. She's deaf too!"

* * *

She had an eighteen-inch waist ... through the middle.

* * *

She was so fat, when she sat around the house, she really sat around the house.

"My girl has the face of an eighteen-year old."

"Tell her to give it back. She's getting it wrinkled."

* * *

She could run naked through the lumber camp and nobody would look up.

* * *

She was so ugly, she used to receive get well cards from Peeping Toms.

* * *

She was so ugly, her folks used to wrap her lunch in a road map.

All the girls in this small town were so ugly, cabbies used to ask *customers* to find them a date.

* * *

She was so ugly, she once wore a see-through dress and nobody did.

* * *

Marsha had a lot of problems in school. All the other girls kept calling her "Big Head! Big Head!" She ran home to her mother. She said, "Mother, all the other kids are making fun of me. They say I have a big head." Her mother held her close and said, "You don't have a big head. You have a normal size head, just like any other child. Now run down to the market and get me ten pounds of potatoes."

"Where'll I carry them?" Marsha asked.

"In your hat, stupid!"

She was listed in the Guinness Book of Yichhh.

* * *

Her face drove some men wild and others out of town.

* * *

What she needed was a kitten—a new puss!

* * *

She's getting prettier every day, but she still has a long way to go.

* * *

Hers was a face as faces go, but one day it went.

"She was worked on by a plastered surgeon."
"You mean, 'plastic.'"
"I mean 'plastered.' You had to be drunk to work on her."

* * *

Her nose came to a point and so did her head.

* * *

She was so ugly, even starvation wouldn't look her in the face.

* * *

She was a professional blind date.

* * *

She was ugly ... even in Braille.

She was so ugly, she used to pass through red lights so the cops would whistle at her.

* * *

"Her lips were like petals."
"Rose petals?"
"No, bicycle pedals."

* * *

Once he saw her, no man could forget her. No matter how hard he tried.

* * *

Man to ugly woman—"I never forget a face, but in your case I'll make an exception."

* * *

She had something that many men want—a mustache.

She had something on her neck that spoiled her looks—her face!

* * *

The man who married her got a prize. He should have gotten a reward.

* * *

She had a little mole on her neck. It was her head.

* * *

She was so ugly as a child that one day she left the house and her parents couldn't find her. They didn't look for her.

* * *

She was so ugly, her parents never had children.

She was so ugly, when she went for life insurance they'd only sell her fire and theft.

* * *

She was so ugly, she went to a coming-out party and they told her to get back in.

* * *

She was so ugly, she sent an application to the Lonely Hearts Club and they wrote back that they weren't that lonely.

* * *

She was so flat-chested, she had to hold her bra up with suspenders.

* * *

She was so flat-chested, her living bra didn't.

She was so ugly, that even though she committed a crime, she was listed on the Ten Most Not Wanted List.

* * *

She gave a new meaning to the word "ugly"—Gruesome!

* * *

Her family had a pet name for her because she looked like one.

* * *

She was so ugly, when she was born the doctor slapped her mother.

He was so ugly, when he was born his mother was arrested for littering.

She was so flat-chested, she had "this side up" tattooed on her bosom in case she ever got lucky.

* * *

She was so ugly, when she was born the doctor didn't slap her. He knew she'd have enough trouble later on.

* * *

"She can't help being ugly."
"I know, but she could stay home more often."

* * *

She was so ugly, in the dictionary under the word "ugly" they put her picture.

She was so ugly, the Wolfman came as her to a Halloween party.

"My wife is so ugly, I only take her out on Halloween."
"Why Halloween?"
"I don't have to explain her."

* * *

She was a cover girl. A manhole cover!

* * *

She used to go to a beauty parlor to get an estimate.

* * *

This young man went to a doctor who examined him and said, "You're anemic." The patient said, "I'd like a second opinion." The doctor said, "You're ugly too."

She was so cross-eyed, when she cried tears rolled down her back.

* * *

She was so ugly, they had to feed her with a whip and a chair.

* * *

This man's wife was so ugly, he took her everywhere he went. It was easier than kissing her goodbye.

* * *

This man came home one night to find a stranger in bed with his ugly wife. The man shrugged his shoulders and said, "I *have* to make love to her. But you?"

She was such an ugly baby the maternity hospital gave her parents a rebate.

* * *

She was so cross-eyed, when she opened one eye all she could see was her other eye.

* * *

She was Lana Turner's sister, Stomach Turner!

* * *

"Do you always talk behind your wife's back?"
"I have to. I can't stand her face."

She was so ugly, she once entered the Miss America contest and was almost deported.

This woman once asked her mirror, "mirror, mirror on the wall, who's the fairest of them all?" She was so ugly, the *wall* broke.

Two men met at a bar. They talked sports, politics, and all the typical subjects of bar talk. Then they started to talk about their wives. Lou, the first man, said that his wife was the ugliest woman in the world. Joe, the other man, insisted that his wife was uglier. They debated through several drinks and finally Lou said, "Have you got some time?"

"Sure," Joe said.

"Good. Then you can come up to my house and take a look at my uggie."

They left the bar, took a taxi, and went to Lou's house. When they got to the living room, Lou said, "Help me put the couch against the wall." The couch was put against the wall. "Now help me roll up the rug." The rug was rolled up. Under it was a heavy trap door. Lou and Joe strained and got the door up. Then Lou called down, "Sylvia, please come up here."

From a cavern down below, a high squeaky voice called up, "Should I throw the flag over my head?" Lou cupped his hands and called down, "No. This man doesn't want to make love to you. He just wants to meet you."

"She has the right to be ugly."
"I know, but she abuses the privilege."

* * *

These two men met at a bar and started to quarrel. One said, "God, you're an ugly s.o.b."

The other said, "And you're drunk."

The first one said, "But I'll be sober in the morning."

* * *

She was such an ugly bride, instead of asking, "Do you take this woman?" the minister said to the groom, "Are you sure?"

* * *

She was such an ugly bride, after the ceremony everybody got in line to kiss the groom.

Her teeth were like stars. They came out at night.

* * *

She was bowlegged and he was knock-kneed. When they stood together they spelled the word, "Ox."

* * *

She was such an ugly strip teaser, when she started to take things off, everybody yelled, "Put it on!"

* * *

He was so skinny, when he went to the beach, dogs buried him.

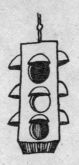

She was so bowlegged, she could get out of both sides of a cab at the same time.

She was so ugly, she could make a train leave the track.

* * *

She was an opera star, one of the ugliest women who ever lived. Ugly, uglier than sin. But when she sang, people forgot her gruesome face and heard only music coming from an angel. One day she got married.

The morning after the honeymoon night, the groom saw her without make-up for the first time. He jumped up and screamed, "Sing something!"

* * *

She came from a town where all the women were ugly. One year, they had a beauty contest and nobody came in first, second or third.

Some women are so ugly, their faces could stop a clock. This woman was so ugly she could stop Switzerland.

* * *

In this small town where the women are ugly and not too well put together, they had a "beautiful legs" contest and a piano won.

* * *

These two men meet. One says, "How would you like a fifty-year-old woman with no shape, an ugly face, hair under her arms, and buck teeth?"
 The other said, "Not too much."
 The first one said, "Then why are you having an affair with my wife?"

* * *

If all women are sisters under the skin, why didn't she go back under and send out a sister?

She was so ugly, when she came into a room, mice jumped on chairs.

* * *

She was so ugly, when she went to the zoo, she had to buy two tickets—one to get in and one to get out.

* * *

If she had been a building, she would have been condemned.

* * *

As a kid, she couldn't play in the sandbox because the cat kept burying her.

* * *

She was so ugly, no tide would bring her in.

She was so ugly, they had to put a pork chop around her neck so the dog would play with her.

His nose was so big, one day he got it stuck in his car, sneezed, and blew his brains out.

* * *

Her face was exactly what it was cracked up to be.

* * *

She's so ugly, she stands in front of a drugstore making people ill.

* * *

She had so much bridgework, every time you kissed her you had to pay a toll charge.

"All she wants is a man who will look up to her."
"Where can you find a midget who needs glasses?"

* * *

Everybody wondered what there was about her right eye that made her left eye keep looking at it.

* * *

When she was at the beauty parlor she looked great, but afterwards she had a problem. She couldn't walk around all day with the mud pack on her face.

* * *

One night she put on a mud pack. When her husband came home, he seeded her.

One day she got a great job. She put on a mud pack and modeled for swamps.

* * *

Even though she had buckteeth, men loved to go out with her. It gave them some place to hang their hats.

* * *

Everybody thought she had buckteeth. Then she went to the dentist and discovered her teeth were straight. She had buckgums.

* * *

"How could she be so ugly for a woman of twenty-five?"
"She gives all of her time to it."

"If you were half a man you'd help me off this bus."
"If you were half a lady you wouldn't need help."

* * *

"Did you hear about my wife?"
"No."
"She ran off with my best friend?"
"I thought I was your best friend."
"Not anymore."

* * *

She was so ugly, her husband went out and took headache lessons.

* * *

"What an ugly woman that old hag is."
"That happens to be my wife."
"I'm sorry."
"Not as sorry as I am."

This coed was kidding her boyfriend, "What are you trying to do, grow a mustache?" He said, "Why not, you did."

* * *

She was so ugly, she could lift a fog.

* * *

He was so ugly, in the army his dog tags came with a collar.

* * *

He was so ugly as a baby, his birth certificate was listed as an accident report.

* * *

She was so fat, when she went to the beach she was a beach.

She had so much hair on her face, she had handlebar eyebrows.

* * *

She used to tweeze her eyebrows . . . if the lawn mower wasn't available.

* * *

He was so ugly, his sister was an only child.

* * *

She was very tall for a woman. She was also very tall for a tree.

* * *

She was so tall, six months a year she went around with snow on her head.

It's very possible that the doctor who came up with the idea of test tube babies had an ugly wife.

* * *

She was so ugly, she was even ugly in the dark.

* * *

"For every woman there's a man."
"If you run into the guy for my wife, have him call collect."

* * *

Her problem was that she was all dressed up and had no face to go.

When she went to the beauty parlor she had to go in through the Emergency Entrance.

* * *

Just the other day she took off twenty pounds . . . her makeup.

* * *

She's so ugly, when she goes to the psychiatrist, he makes her lie on the couch face down.

* * *

A fat man is only a little boy gone to waist.

* * *

She had a lot of hidden charms, so one day they decided to look for them. They held a scavenger hunt.

She was so bowlegged, she had to wear industrial strength pantyhose.

* * *

Her bra was so padded, one day she threw it down and it bounced out of the bedroom window.

* * *

Everyday he prayed that his brother lived. If his brother died, then he'd be the ugliest man in the world.

* * *

The space between her breasts was called Silicone Valley.

One day she wore feathers. She was attacked by an ostrich.

* * *

They called her a hot potato. She was built like one.

* * *

She was so fat, she had to use an expandable hula hoop.

* * *

She was so fat, she could make a hula hoop cry.

His nose was so big, at a bus stop he could shelter eight people from the rain.

* * *

When she wiggled her ears, she had to hold onto something so she wouldn't take off.

* * *

At her church group she went out for their production of "Peter Pan." She didn't get the part because her pan had petered out.

* * *

She was so ugly, her obscene phone calls came collect.

She always went around in a permanent wave—her nose.

* * *

"He's a very ugly guy. How'd he get such a pretty wife?"
"Well, one day he opened his wallet and there she was."

* * *

She was so knock-kneed, her legs walk single file.

* * *

A very fat man was experiencing a great deal of trouble having sex with his wife. His stomach stuck way out and he was unable to see the paraphernalia by which a man consummates the sex act. One night he came home late and found his wife standing on her head. "What's that for?" he asked. She said, "I figured tonight you could drop in."

She was so ugly, she could scare a saint out of a thicket.

* * *

A man was unfortunate enough to have five extremely ugly daughters. Each night when he came home from work, he'd see his youngest sitting watching television. He'd smile at her and say, "I wish I had two just like you." He did this night after night.

Finally, the ugly daughter became curious. She said, "Dad, I know I'm gruesome. Yet you come home and look at me and say, "I wish I had two exactly like you. Why?"

The father answered, "Because I've got *five* like you."

* * *

She had a very big dimple. It would have looked nice except her face kept falling into it.

She had an hourglass figure, but the sand kept dripping out.

* * *

She had such a terrible figure, when she took a physical, she kept her clothes on and the *doctor* got undressed.

* * *

She was so ugly, on her cheek she had a beauty question mark.

* * *

Everytime he saw his wife with a broom he didn't know whether she was about to clean or take a ride.

She was so fat, as a child when she got off the merry-go-round her horse limped.

"There's really not much difference between ugly women and beautiful women."
"Great. Let's go after the beautiful ones."

* * *

An ugly woman had a car accident. The car was totalled. Police rushed to the scene. One policeman said, "What should we do with the wreck?"
 The other policeman said, "We'll get all the details and then we'll drive her home."

* * *

She wore so many mud packs, grass grew on her chin.

* * *

"Am I some kind of animal? Trash? Garbage? Junk?"
"Keep going. You're getting close."

A shipwrecked man rushed to the water's edge to see what the small bobbing object was. Grabbing it, he saw that it was a wine bottle with a French label from the year 1907. He fondled the bottle with both hands. Suddenly the cork popped off and a genie appeared.

However, it was one of the ugliest genies ever fantasized. Her body was scraggly and misshapen. Her face looked as if it had scraped bottom for years.

The man looked at the genie, puzzled. "Genies are supposed to be gorgeous and have beautiful figures."

The genie answered, "1907 was a bad year for genies."

* * *

"If you touch me, I'll call the cops."
"They won't touch you either."

* * *

Her husband looked into the face of death—hers.

She looked like a gold digger . . . a miner!

* * *

One day she sent a picture of her body through the mails. They sent it right to the dead letter office.

* * *

"Take my money, my diamonds, my body."
"Can I take two out of three?"

* * *

She was so skinny, every time she got sunburned her back peeled.

* * *

She was such an ugly bride, instead of a wedding ring, her beau gave her a platinum setting for her wart.

She was a real homebody. Nobody would take her out of it.

* * *

She went out to sell her body, but she was so ugly they sent her to a rummage sale.

* * *

She was so ugly, she couldn't lure anybody out of a burning building.

* * *

His second wife was so ugly that two weeks before he brought her home he told his children ghost stories so they wouldn't be frightened when they saw her.

She was human mace.

* * *

She was so ugly, when an artist was painting her portrait her face broke his brush.

* * *

She weighed two hundred pounds on the hoof, which was what she had instead of feet.

* * *

When she came to town, rapists turned themselves in.

* * *

He was so fat, when he went to New York City, they wanted to make him another borough

She was born in the Crash of 1929. That was the year her doctor dropped her.

* * *

People kept telling her she had such beautiful wavy hair. Then they found out her hair was straight. Her scalp was wavy. When she went for a permanent, the beautician would ask, "One lump or two?"

* * *

She was so ugly, her face could curdle a cow. She went to a farm one day. For the next two weeks the cows gave yogurt.

* * *

Her face was so oily, Arabs followed her.

Her front teeth were so far apart, they asked for severance pay.

* * *

She was so bloated, twice a day her body went out with the tide.

* * *

He was so ugly, he got into the army as a war atrocity.

* * *

One habit gave her away. She liked to nip at a stranger's heels.

She was such an ugly bride, on their honeymoon the groom insisted on separate rooms ... in different hotels ... in different cities.

* * *

"Ravage me."
"I can't. Nature beat me to it."

* * *

Always an obedient wife, the bank robber's wife did as she was told and put a stocking over her head. Then one day, she realized he didn't take her on any jobs.

* * *

She had a well-knit face ... with several runs.

At the school dance she was always a wallflower. Then one day somebody watered her.

* * *

She had crow's feet. Not on her eyes. These were the kind of feet she had.

* * *

She had ten fingers, just like any normal person . . . seven and three.

* * *

She was some dish . . . a main dish at a luau.

There she was, lying on soft white satin sheets. A vampire appeared in the open window. He went to her side. He looked at her face. He leaned over and bit the bed.

* * *

"I took Frankenstein to see my wife."
"There must have been a lot of screaming."
"I thought he'd never stop."

* * *

She had something that could melt a man—her breath.

* * *

"My boyfriend has terrible dandruff."
"Give him Head and Shoulders."
"Really. But how do you give shoulders?"

She was so fat, when she'd sit down in the nude, she'd suction herself to the seat.

She had so many wrinkles, she used to mark her face with a bookmark so she could find her mouth.

* * *

A compliment for a young lady—"You don't sweat too much for a fat broad."

* * *

Even though she was ugly, her husband adored her. He even bought her a diamond for her leash.

* * *

"Ravage me," the ugly damsel said to the dragon. The dragon looked at her. "Don't we dragons have a bad enough reputation?"

They called her Dragonlady. Half her body was dragging on the floor.

* * *

She was so ugly, she had to go to the Sunday tea dance on Tuesday.

* * *

He kissed her on the neck. He kissed her on the chin. Then he kissed her on the next chin. And the next chin. And the next.
    Finally he said, "Let me know when I'm getting near a lip."

* * *

She has everything a woman has. Except they gave her a child's portion.

She was so lonely, at night she used to walk her wig.

* * *

When she went camping, the bears built a fire to keep her away.

* * *

She didn't shave her legs much. Most of the time she just put them up in curlers.

* * *

The last time she heard a whistle, she was hit by a train.

* * *

She was the kind who traded on her looks ... at garage sales.

She was so fat, when she walked down the street in slacks, it looked like two puppies fighting under a blanket.

* * *

She was as ugly as three miles of scar.

* * *

She was a real rockin' chick. That's what they threw at her.

* * *

When it came to looks, men gave her the seal of approval, but the seals objected.

* * *

He was so skinny, his back pockets were in his other pants.

He was so skinny, the crease in his pants was him.

* * *

He was so skinny, he had to keep his navel on a watch fob.

* * *

She looked like the den mother for the Dirty Dozen.

* * *

With his wife, he was a man of few words . . . "Fetch. Sit."

* * *

Men loved to travel with her. She was an overnight bag.

The gardener's wife had a nice figure, but one day it went to pot.

* * *

She was like a great Russian book. But nobody could figure out if her face was the crime or the punishment.

* * *

"Her beauty is down real deep."
"She must have a gorgeous skeleton."

* * *

She had a fragile beauty. That was marked on the box she came in. Unfortunately, it was dropped.

She was so ugly, when she went on a picnic, ants didn't.

* * *

His nose was so big, it had its own heart and lungs.

* * *

She was such an ugly bride, the hotel gave them the honeymoon sour.

* * *

She was so ugly, when she called Dial-a-Prayer, they said they couldn't help.

* * *

She was so ugly, when she called information, they told her to get a face lift.

He went through medical school . . . as a cadaver.

* * *

"Wow, she has a face like a rhinocerous."
"Not only that. Once a month she gets an urge to ram a jeep."

* * *

She's so ugly, even her answering service won't answer.

* * *

She inspired a great book—*The Naked and the Dead*.

* * *

Ugly girls are a dime a dozen. Some are so ugly, the won't sell at half that price.

She's so ugly, they have towels made out to Him and What.

The King of the Lower Nile and the King of the Upper Nile ran into each other one day. After comparing great accomplishments, the King of the Lower Nile said, "Look, we got all the pyramids we'll need. And all the sphinxes. And we've collected gorgeous women for years. Let's try to collect something different."

"Like what?"

"Let's see who can come up with the ugliest woman in the world."

"What a great idea. Okay, one year from today, let's meet and see who wins. We'll bet a million Nile dollars."

"Done."

So the kings departed, each for his own castle.

The next morning, they called in their ministers and told them about the bet. Each king insisted that he win. Cost was no object.

For the next twenty years, details were sent out all over the civilized world. Word would come about an ugly woman on top of a high mountain. In ten minutes an expedition would start.

If word came from some remote oasis, men mounted their camels and braved the searing heat. Men died by the dozens from starvation. Men perished from the lack of water.

For three hundred and sixty-four days, the hunts went on. Finally, at the cost of ten thousand men on each side and hundreds of millions of dollars, entries were found.

The two kings gathered at a cool spot along the river.

Both women were paraded before the huge throng. Both were ugly, among the ugliest creatures of all time, and caused viewers to faint and gag. Finally, it was decided that the King of the Lower Nile had one. "All right," he said to the King of the Upper Nile, "give me my million dollars. I won."

The King of the Upper Nile looked at him stunned. "You won? I thought we were playing two out of three."

* * *

"Look at the ugly woman over there. She must have a hundred wrinkles on her face."
"It's more like two hundred."
"Look close, it's more like three hundred."
"You know, this is a nice game, let's play a nickle a hundred."

She was so hairy, when she asked for a mink coat, her husband only had to put sleeves on her body.

* * *

She was so fat, when she went into the ocean nobody else could use it at the same time.

* * *

She was so ugly, in church they put her on the other side of the curtain even if she wasn't confessing.

* * *

She was so ugly, she was in some of those "before" and "after" headache remedy commercials. She played "during."

She was a benevolent woman ... she looked like an Elk.

* * *

Her rear end was so big, she had to have a girdle for each cheek.

* * *

He was so fat, one time he got on a scale and a little card came out and said, "Gimme a break, I'm only a scale."

* * *

She was so fat, when she got married, instead of her father, a crane had to give her away.

He was so ugly, at his wedding, *he* wore the veil.

* * *

This ugly wife kept badgering her husband that even with her ugliness she'd outlive him. She said, "I'll dance on your grave." He said, "Great, I'll be buried at sea."

* * *

She had thirty-two beautiful white teeth ... and that was just on top.

* * *

She was kind of heavy, but when men went out with her they had a whale of a time.

"My girl has no bosom."
"That's nothing."
"Oh, you've seen her."

* * *

She was a regular cave woman ... that's where they kept her.

* * *

"My girl is a knockout."
"Is she that pretty?"
"No, she's just a good boxer."

* * *

They wanted to put her in the ring, because she looked like a boxer.

Very ashamed of her gigantic bust, a woman went to a faith healer. He looked at her and said that faith could move mountains. So he prayed. Her breasts became smaller and absolutely beautiful. But now she has two large lumps on her rear end.

* * *

"What a colorful sofa your uncle has."
"That's not a sofa. That's my aunt."

* * *

"Is that a picture of your fiancee?"
"Yup."
"Gee, I wish I knew a rich girl."

* * *

When she posed for her graduation album, she didn't have to pose with the rest of the class for a group picture. She *was* a group picture.

"Was your girlfriend's diet a success?"
"Was it! She disappeared completely last Tuesday."

* * *

It was a good thing for her that a mirror can't laugh.

* * *

A woman was unhappy that she looked like a little old lady. She went to a plastic surgeon who performed his magic on her. She didn't look like a little old lady anymore. She looked like a little old man.

* * *

She dyed her hair so often she slept in a vat.

"Beauty is only skin deep."
"Too bad it's so near and you can't get close to it."

* * *

She was a suicide blonde ... dyed by her own hands.

* * *

She wore a bra, out of hope.

* * *

He wasn't fat. It's just that he was wide-shoudered from the hips down.

* * *

She had a rare beauty. Nobody could find it.

She parted her hair sideways. Dates went crazy whispering into her nose.

* * *

She was ugly, it looked as if she had been born right into a wall at high speed.

* * *

She was as cute as a button. She had four holes in her face.

* * *

People looked at her and wondered where the organ grinder was.

* * *

"Why don't you take your wife to the zoo?"
"If they want her, let them come for her."

There was dew on her lips and dew in her eyes. That's what she was—"dew-dew."

* * *

"Look at that broad. She is ugly, ugly."
"You know, she's a hooker."
"Who would pay to go with her?"
"Mostly men who are trying to cut down."

* * *

For five years she worked in a brothel. Her average price was fifty dollars. Of course, some men wanted more.

* * *

At her wedding she wore something blue—her veins.

"She didn't invent ugliness."
"I know, but she may be the local distributor for it."

* * *

She had a joke face. She made people gag.

* * *

If there are so many beautiful brides and grooms, where do all the ugly married couples come from?

* * *

She was so ugly, her passport pictures came out *nice.*

She looked like a loser in a cockfight. When she heard what they were saying, she got insulted. Because she'd won.

* * *

She was so ugly, her makeup came in a snakebite kit.

* * *

She knew her oats, because that's what they fed her.

* * *

She was so ugly, she entered an "ugly" contest and came in first, second, and third. She would have come in fourth too, but that entry was the judge's sister.

The stork who brought her resigned the next day and went into wading.

* * *

She set men on fire. She gave them heartburn.

* * *

She was so ugly, customs wouldn't let her enter the country without a crate.

* * *

When she met a man she'd heave her bosom. Most of them would throw it back.

* * *

"She's pretty as a picture."
"Let's hang her."

She's so ugly, it looks as if the stork made a crash landing.

This woman went to her psychiatrist. "I'm ugly," she said. "Everybody says I'm the ugliest woman in the world."

The psychiatrist answered softly, "You're not ugly. You're not ugly. But next Friday's Halloween, would you like to sit in my window?"

* * *

They were neighbors. Ten times a day she passed his door. He appreciated that.

* * *

Some men are fat and ugly, but not him. He's skinny and ugly.

* * *

She had what it took, but she'd had it so long, nobody wanted it.

She looked like a million, every year of it.

* * *

She could have been a calendar girl, but she couldn't get any dates.

* * *

She was a girl right out of the Old South. She had a shape like a bale of cotton.

* * *

She was such an ugly baby, the stork had her sent by mail.

This man wakes up at dawn and finds that he is in a very strange room. Next to him lies the ugliest woman in the world. Her face is misshapen, her nose goes in ten directions, her skin pockmarked. She is a total uggie. The man gets out of bed, gets dressed, and reaches into his pocket for a twenty-dollar bill, which he puts down on the night table. As he starts out of the strange place, he passes the bathroom. At the open bathroom door stands a woman even uglier than the one in bed. She looks at him and says, "Nothing for the bridesmaid?"

* * *

She weighed two hundred pounds, but that was a round figure.

* * *

The day she was born her father threw rocks at the stork.

He looked like the first husband of a widow.

* * *

She's had a face that looked as if it had worn out five bodies.

* * *

She's had so many facelifts, when she raises her eyebrows, she pulls up her stockings.

* * *

When men looked at her time stood still. She could stop a clock.

* * *

She weighed a hundred and plenty.

* * *

She went to Weight Watchers. They told her to wait.

* * *

He was so ugly that he once won a French Medal of Honor, but they couldn't find a general brave enough to kiss him.

Her soldier boyfriend won a medal for bravery above and beyond the call of duty. He was seen in public with her.

* * *

She's so ugly, her phone doesn't even ring when she's in the shower.

* * *

She was very superstitious. She had a rabbit's foot . . . and one that was normal.

* * *

A very fat woman got on a bus. "Isn't anybody going to offer me a seat?"
One little fellow raised his hand, "I'm willing to make a contribution."

* * *

When her parents left her on somebody's doorstep, they were arrested for littering.

* * *

They hung her and kissed the mistletoe.

She looked as if she'd been beaten with an ugly stick.

* * *

She was so bowlegged, she had to get out of bed at night to turn around.

* * *

She has a Supreme Court figure—no appeal.

* * *

"Get ready to die. I'm going to shoot you."
"Why?"
"I always said I'd shoot anybody who looked like me."
"Do I look like you?"
"Yup."
"Then shoot."

Her teeth are so bucked, when she smiles she combs her mustache.

* * *

"Your wife looks a little heavier around the hips."
"Since the earthquake, she's settling."

* * *

"What a strange-looking man."
"Sir, that happens to be my daughter."
"I'm sorry. I didn't know you were her mother."
"I'm her father."

* * *

He never worried about his baldness; he was born that way.

"Dad, are you getting taller?"
"Why, son?"
"Your head seems to be peaking through your hair."

* * *

"Listen, there's a fly at the end of your nose. Why don't you brush it off?"
"Why don't you?"
"Why me?"
"You're closer to it."

* * *

She was definitely not two-faced or she would have worn the other one.

* * *

This woman got on a broken scale as two young children walked by. The scale read 120 pounds. One of the kids turned to the other, "Gee, that lady is hollow."

He was so fat, one time he got up in a bus and gave his seat to four ladies.

* * *

"Officer, can you see me across the street?"
"Lady, I could see you a mile away."

* * *

She was so ugly, when she kissed her lover she kept her eyes closed so she wouldn't see him suffer.

* * *

The police are still looking for the stork that brought her.

* * *

On her birthday, her father goes to the zoo and throws rocks at the stork.

If she sued her face for slander she could collect.

* * *

She looked as if she'd gone out Halloween night and forgot to come back.

* * *

She looked like a character witness for a nightmare.

* * *

Her tongue was so long, she could lick an envelope after it was in the mailbox.

* * *

She was so ugly, she could turn a cannibal into a vegetarian.

He was tall and she was fat. When they made love, it looked like an exclamation point.

* * *

She was a covergirl. When a guy met her, he ran for cover.

* * *

She was not very photogenic, especially in person.

* * *

Although she looked like a chimp, nobody wanted to monkey around with her.

* * *

She looked like a real dog, but not even a Doberman would pinch her.

* * *

"There's a man out there with a wooden leg named Smith."
"Really? What's the name of his other leg?"

"Which one is yours?"

THE AUTHOR

A well-known comedy writer who has worked for such shows as "The Dean Martin Show," "Trapper John," and "Too Close for Comfort," Milt Rosen has all the credentials.

He has written material for almost every great comedian from Bob Hope to Milton Berle. He has worked on record albums for Bob Newhart and The Smothers Brothers. His routine about Sir Walter Raleigh teaching the English about tobacco has become a standard. Many of his jokes have become a part of the language of comedy. Over the years he has done as many "roasts" as any writer alive, including roastings of famous political and sports figures.

A father, husband, and generally a nice person, Milt has written six books. One of them, a novel about Hollywood spiced generously with sex, is used as a textbook on filth at many leading universities. His latest, the story of his tempestuous love affair with Indira Gandhi in Philadelphia, is soon to be issued on a madras shirt.

Mr. Rosen ca be contacted at any 7-11 in the San Fernando Valley where he teaches Beginning Armed Robbery. In addition, he can often be found at the Northridge, California Art Museum where he is trying to repair the picture frame so the museum can open.